# LIONS AND TIGERS

**Design**
David West
Children's Book Design
**Illustrations**
Tessa Barwick
**Picture Research**
Cecilia Weston-Baker
**Editor**
Denny Robson
**Consultant**
John Stidworthy



*Designed and produced by*
Aladdin Books Ltd
70 Old Compton Street
London W1

*First published in the United States in 1988 by*
Gloucester Press
387 Park Avenue South
New York NY 10016

Printed in Belgium

ISBN 0-531-17101-9
Library of Congress Catalog
Card Number 88-50511

This book tells you about lions and tigers – where they live, what they eat and how they survive. Find out some surprising facts about them in the boxes on each page. The identification chart at the back will help you when you see lions and tigers in zoos or wildlife parks.

The little square shows you the size of the animal. Each side represents 3 m (10 ft).

**The picture opposite shows a young male Indian tiger**

FIRST SIGHT

# LIONS AND TIGERS

Lionel Bend

GLOUCESTER PRESS

New York · London · Toronto · Sydney

# Introduction

There are 35 different species of cats. The lion and the tiger are the biggest. All cats are hunters and meat-eaters. Lions live mainly in Africa, where they are found in open grassland and sometimes in desert and bush country. Tigers live in India and parts of China, the Soviet Union and the Far East. They prefer forest country. However, in the north of their range tigers live in snow-covered pine forests, and in the south they live in hot jungles.

Like other mammals, lions and tigers are intelligent and care for their young. But they are also very fierce animals and behave quite differently from their close relative, the domestic cat.

**Contents**



◁ **A male lion with its wildebeest prey**

# Big cats

Lions and tigers are both "big cats." This is a group of the cat family that also includes the Leopard, Snow Leopard and the Jaguar. A domestic cat measures about 70 cm (28 in) from nose to tip of tail and weighs around 4 kg (9 lb). A lion can measure up to 3 m (10 ft) in length and weigh up to 240 kg (520 lb). A tiger can grow to 3.6 m (12 ft) and 350 kg (770 lb). Male lions and tigers grow 25 per cent bigger than females.

Like all cats, lions and tigers have strong muscles for running and jumping, and sharp teeth and claws for gripping and tearing their prey. But big cats have particularly large heads. They also roar rather than yowl and purr only as they breathe out.

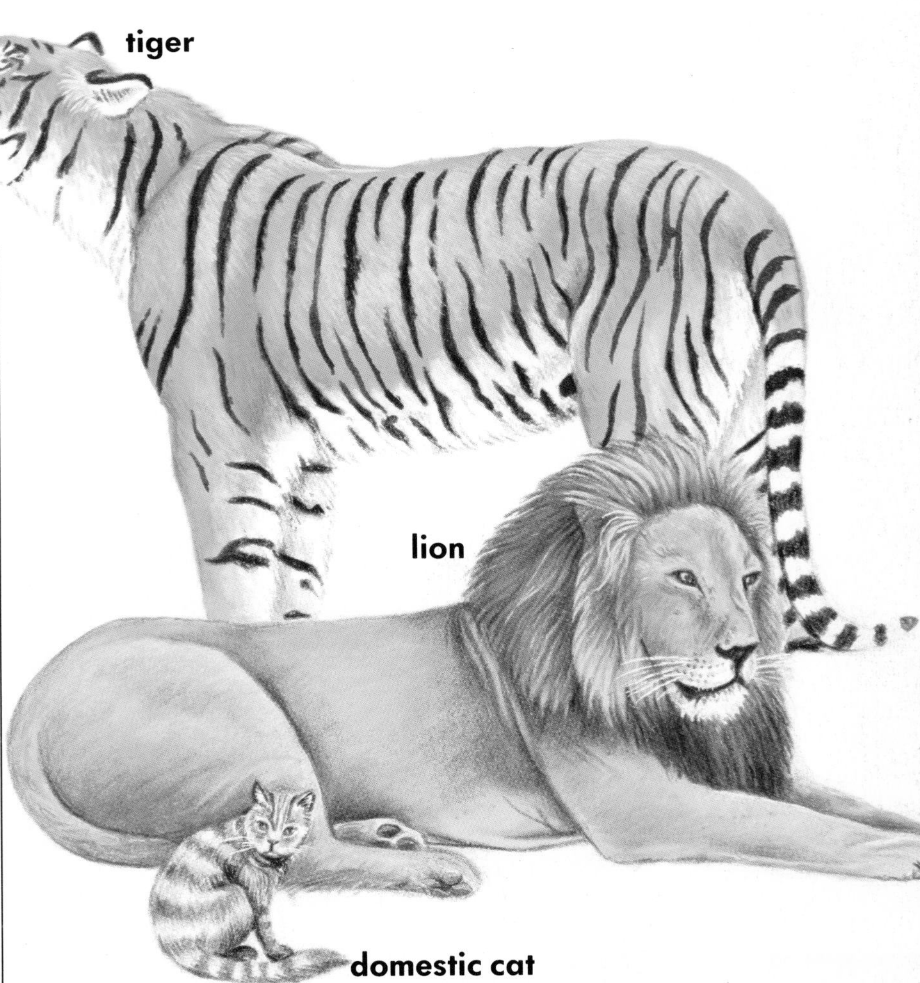


Saber-toothed tigers lived 25 to 2 million years ago. They used their huge front upper teeth, or fangs, to pierce the necks of their victims. They had fangs 20 cm (8 in) long and used to kill elephants.

◁ **The tiger's stripes help it blend into its forest home**

◁ A pride of lions resting in the shade

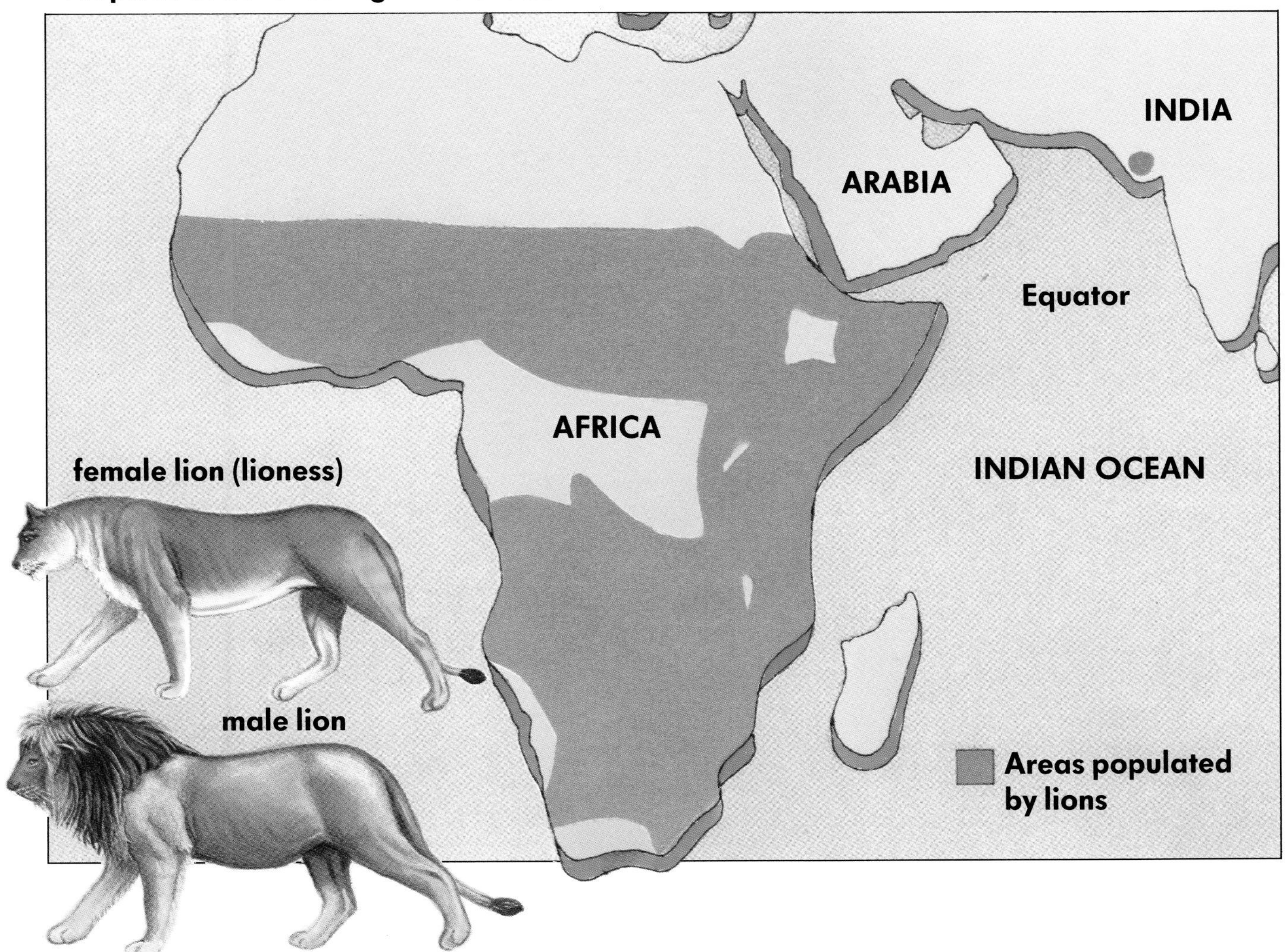


# Lion – King of Beasts

The lion is often called the King of Beasts. An adult male lion is larger than most meat-eaters and is much larger than any person. It has a long, stately mane of thick fur around its neck and its often calm nature adds to its majestic appearance.

The lion is the only cat that lives in groups. Sometimes a male lion may travel alone or in a small group with other males. But lions love company. They live together in prides. These are usually made up of a few adult males, ten or more adult female lions and their young. The males defend the pride's feeding and resting areas. They also prevent male lions of other prides from mating with their females.

An Indian tiger swimming in a river ▷

# Tiger – Lord of the Jungle

The tiger is the lion's closest relative. Only a few thousand years ago, these two animals lived side by side across central southern Asia and India. Today the tiger is most common in northern India.

Tigers vary in size and color from place to place. The biggest tiger, the Siberian, can reach 3.9 m (13 ft) in length. It has a yellowish coat that is tinged with red in the summer. The coat is also very thick, which keeps the animal warm in the cold winters. The smallest tiger, the Sumatran, grows to about 2.5 m (8 ft) long. It has a reddish-yellow coat with thin, closely set stripes. The tiger's coat helps it blend in with the foliage and dry grass of its home.

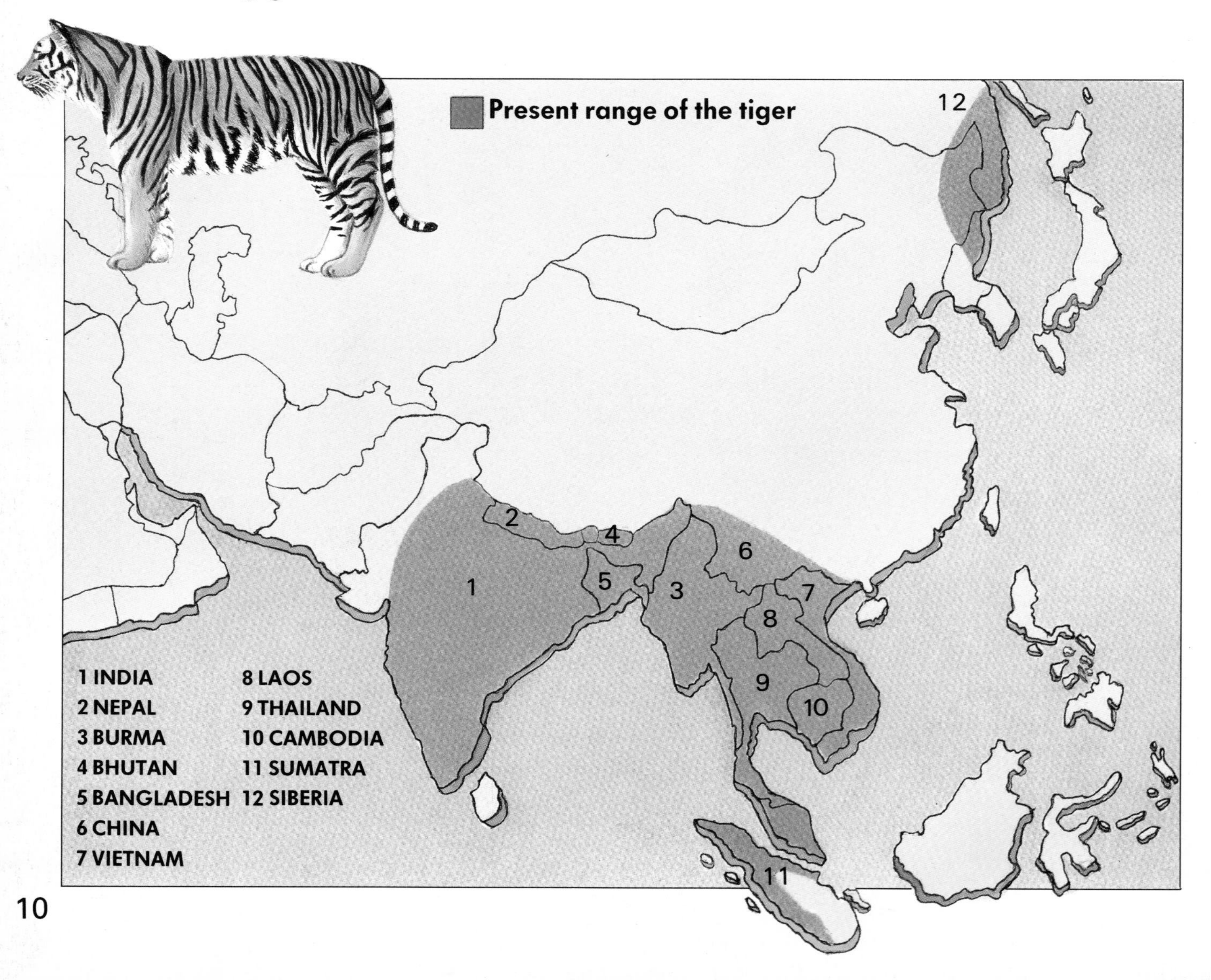

# Teeth and claws

Lions and tigers are expert hunters. They use their teeth and claws as killing weapons. Their jaws are short and powerful, which gives them great biting strength. Cats have 30 teeth. The biggest are the upper canines, the fangs, which are used for grabbing and piercing. The incisors, the front teeth, are small but sharp. They are used for making a nip in the skin of prey. The side  or cheek teeth are used like scissors to slice off lumps of meat to swallow.

Like all cats, lions and tigers have soft pads of skin on their paws so they can creep up silently on their prey. The paws have claws for gripping and tearing flesh. The animals scratch at trees to sharpen their claws.

Lions and tigers can pull back their claws inside sheaths, folds of skin, between their toes. The claws are extended only when the animals pounce to kill.

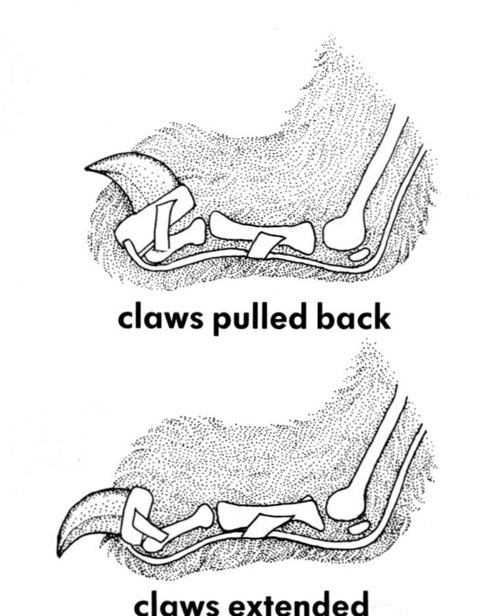

claws pulled back

claws extended

**Head of a lioness, showing strong skull and teeth**

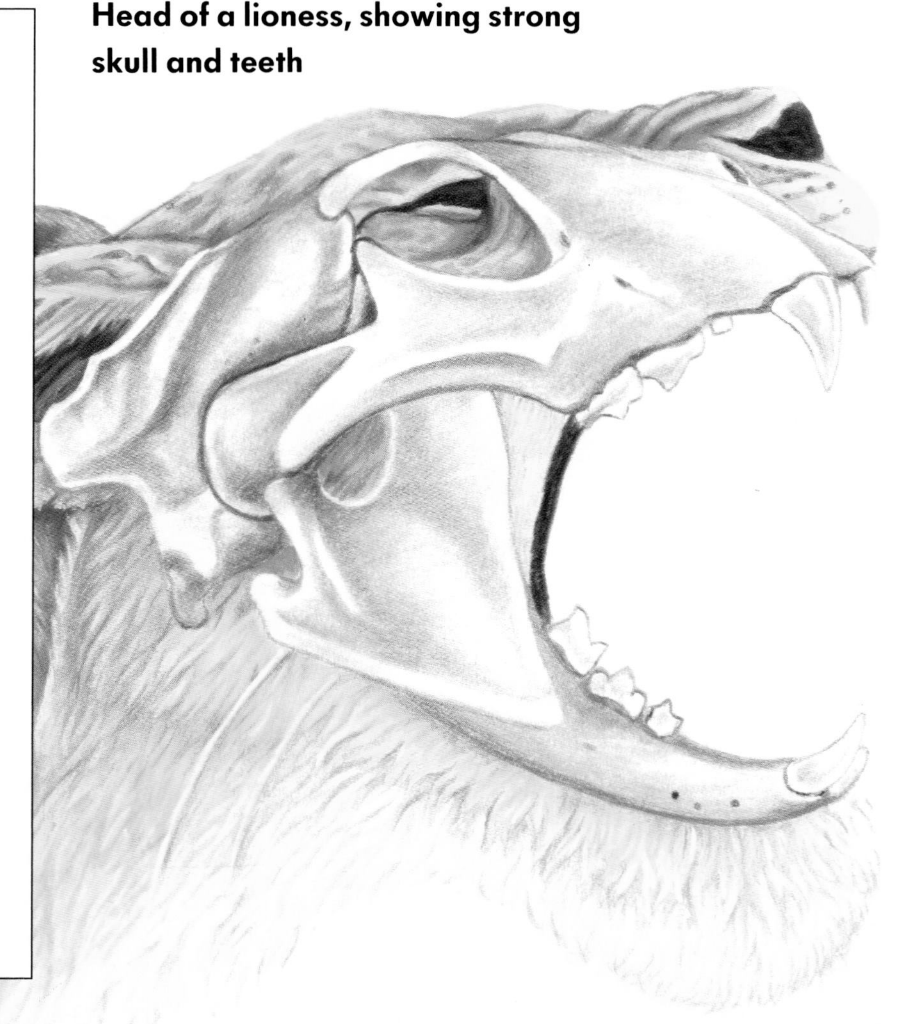

# Catching prey

Lions that live in open grassland, where there is little cover to hide in, often hunt at night and in groups. Lions that live among tangled bush often hunt by day, and then alone or in pairs. Usually the adult lionesses do the hunting. They are lighter in weight than the males and therefore more agile and faster moving. Also, without a mane, they are less easily seen and can wrestle better in close combat. Often several lionesses hunt together. They spread out and surround the prey. Then, when they are about 30 m (100 ft) from the prey, they attack.

Tigers hunt alone and at night. Sometimes a tiger waits for its prey near a waterhole. Then it creeps up on the animal. With a quick dash, it rushes at its victim, knocks it to the ground, and grabs the animal's neck with its mighty jaws.

Big cats kill their prey by biting and squeezing the victim's throat. This means the animal cannot breathe, and so it dies quickly without a struggle.

**A lioness attacking a wildebeest**

A tigress feeding on a deer ▷

# Food and feeding

An adult lion or tiger needs about 15 kg (33 lb) of meat a day. A lion hunts only when it must eat, and then takes one animal at a time. It kills one or two large animals each week. A tiger will kill several animals if it can, but feeds on only one or two of them. Many of the kills are eaten by wild dogs and other tigers.

All members of a lion's pride share a kill. The prey is eaten on the spot or is dragged to a place where it can be guarded. The adult males eat first, then the females and young. A tiger pulls its victim into cover before feeding. When it has eaten enough, it hides the kill by putting grass or earth over it. It returns to the carcass for several days to feed.

**The lioness kills prey and drags it to the pride.**

**The male lions eat first . . .**

Lions eat mainly wildebeest, gazelle, waterbuck and zebra. Tigers eat deer, wild pigs and water buffalo. Where they live near farms they also eat sheep and goats.

**. . . then the lionesses and cubs eat.**

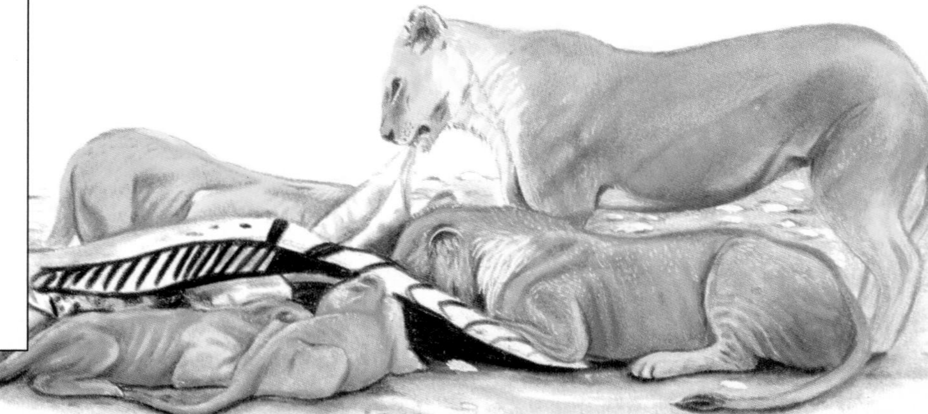

# Family life

Within a pride of lions, the adult females are usually sisters, cousins or mothers and daughters. Each may have several young. The adult males are often brothers, but are not close relatives of the other pride members. Male lions are driven out of a pride when they are about three years old. They often live alone for a year or two, then compete with other adult males to take over a pride and become its leaders or defenders.

A typical tiger family consists of a mother tiger and her one or two young. The young leave the family when they are about two and a half years old. Adult male tigers mostly live alone. They share the company of female tigers only at mating time.

Young adult male lions that have just taken over a pride may kill cubs already in the pride. They then mate with the females. This means only their own young grow to be adults.

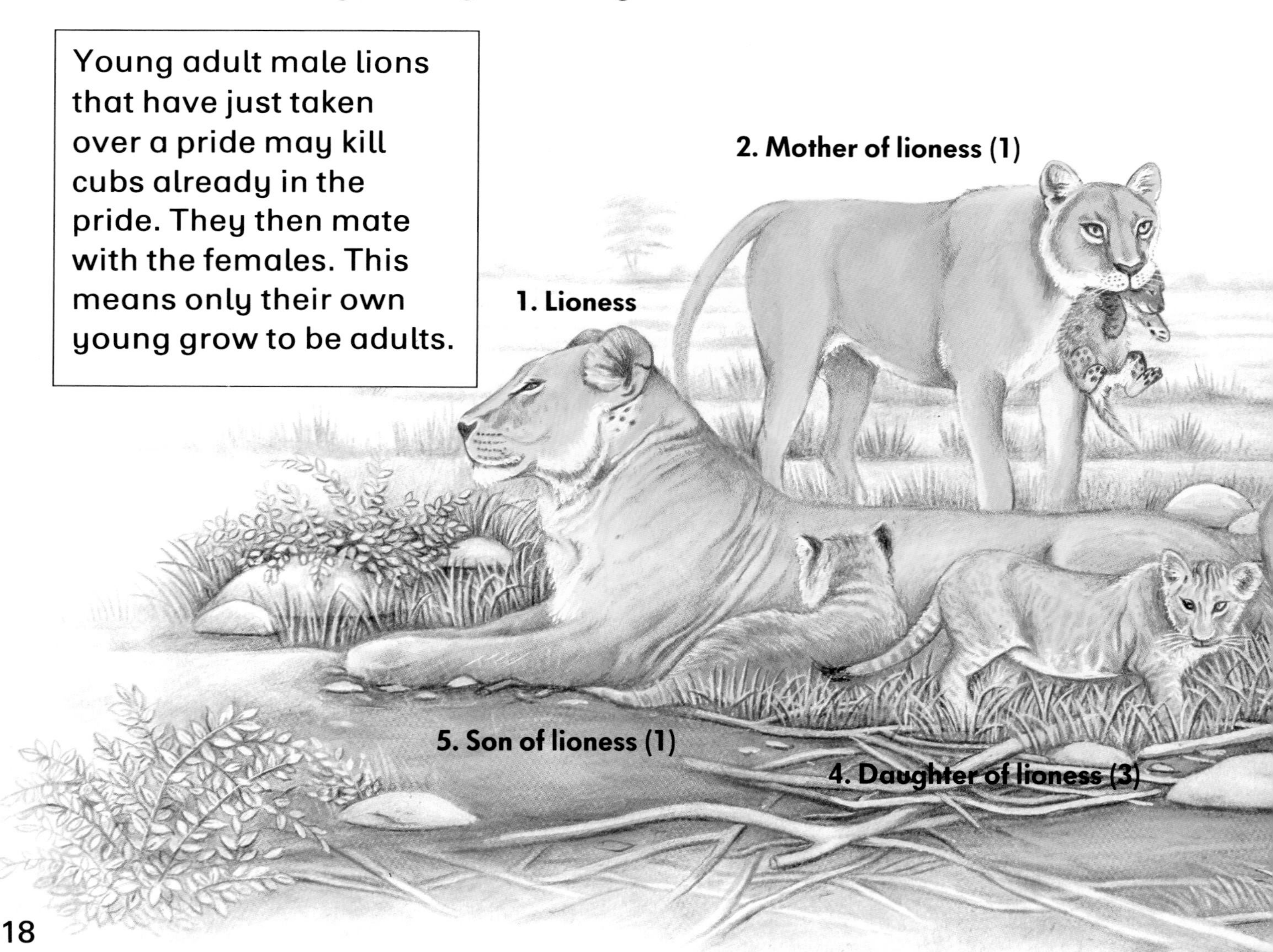

A tigress with her cubs

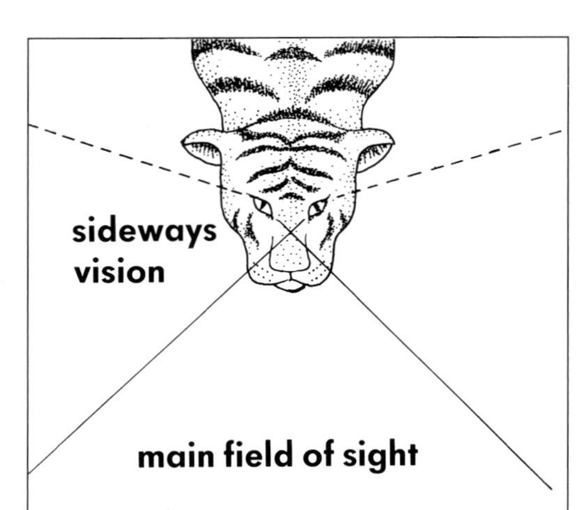


The eyes of lions and tigers face forward, allowing them to judge distances accurately when hunting. This is most important when they are about to spring at prey.

**A male tiger wrinkles its lips on smelling a female that is ready to mate.**

# Senses and scents

In daylight, lions and tigers can see about as well as we can. But at night, when they usually hunt, their sight is six times better than ours. Their ear flaps are large and can move around to collect sounds from most directions. The whiskers around their mouths are long, stiff and very sensitive to touch. They are especially useful for finding a way through grass at night without making a sound.

These big cats use their senses of smell and taste mostly for sniffing and tasting the scents of one another. Males will sniff out females at mating time and all adults use body scents and urine to mark out their territories.

**A lion sprays a bush to mark its territory** ▷

# Territories

A tiger sometimes travels 10 km (6 miles) in a single night in search of food and water. In a year it may move over an area of 150 sq km (58 sq miles), which is known as the animal's territory. Occasionally, the tiger meets other tigers whose territories cross its own. Each animal then marks the edge of its territory. It uses its strong-smelling urine and dung, and also rubs scent from glands under its chin on twigs and branches.

Lion prides also have territories. Where food is easy to find, territories may measure only 20 sq km (8 sq miles). When prides meet, the adults may roar loudly at one another. Adult males from each pride also fight to defend their home areas or females and young.

**Male lions fight to defend their territories**

**Two Indian tigers lash out at each other with their paws ▷**

# Courtship

Male and female lions are able to breed when they are about three to four years old. Pregnancy lasts for about 16 weeks in both lions and tigers. Lions may mate at any time of the year. However, female tigers mate only when their cubs can be born at a time when there is plenty of prey.

The female is willing to mate on only two or three days during each breeding season. At this time the males often fight with one another for the chance to mate with a female. The winner then approaches the female. At first the two animals growl and snarl, but then they rub heads and lick each other before mating. Males often mate with many females.

**A male lion grabs a female's neck during courtship**

**Male and female tigers rub heads before mating** ▷

# Growing up

A pregnant lioness or tigress usually gives birth to two or three cubs. At birth, the cubs measure about 60 cm (24 in) from head to tip of tail and weigh 1-2 kg (2-4 lbs). The mother leaves the cubs in a hiding place each time she hunts. But often the cubs are found and killed by hyenas and other predators.

The cubs feed on their mother's milk until they are about three months old, then they start to eat meat. They are not strong enough to fend for themselves until they are about two. Their mother then has her next litter of cubs and loses interest in her first offspring. The young adults begin their independent lives. Lions and tigers live for about 15 to 20 years.

**Young Sumatran tiger cubs**

**Lion cubs feeding on their mother's milk** ▷

# Survival file

Lions and tigers have suffered greatly from human activity. Many thousands have been killed over the past hundred years, either for sport or to provide fur coats or rugs. Occasionally, when a lion or tiger is desperate for food, it will kill farm animals or even people. This can be a reason to destroy the animal. But many of these beatiful animals are trapped or poisoned simply because they *might* be dangerous. There are strict laws about hunting lions and tigers, but poaching and illegal trading still go on.

**Tiger skins are still sold in shops in some countries**

Today, the greatest threat to these big cats is the spread of villages and farms into their natural homes. In parts of Africa and India, places have been set aside as reserves for lions and tigers. There they can roam and hunt freely. In some reserves, populations of lions and tigers have increased. But throughout Africa, the long-term survival of lions is doubtful. And the most common type of tiger, the Indian, numbers no more than about 3,500. Eighty years ago there were 40,000.

**This electrified wooden man scares off tigers**

**Lions and tigers breed in Safari Parks**

Another threat to the survival of lions and tigers is the reduction in the amount of food they have available. Zebras, gazelles, buffaloes, wildebeest and deer are the major prey of big cats. These animals are killed in large numbers by people, either for food or to protect crops.

However, in zoos and wildlife parks around the world, lions and tigers are being bred successfully. Scientists no longer need to take animals from the wild to study them. And we do not have to trample over their homelands to see them.

# Identification chart

This chart will help you identify the different types of tiger alive today and to compare the size and appearance of an adult male and an adult female lion when you see them in a zoo, wildlife park or nature reserve. Each square represents 1.3m (4ft). Different types of tigers live in different parts of the world.

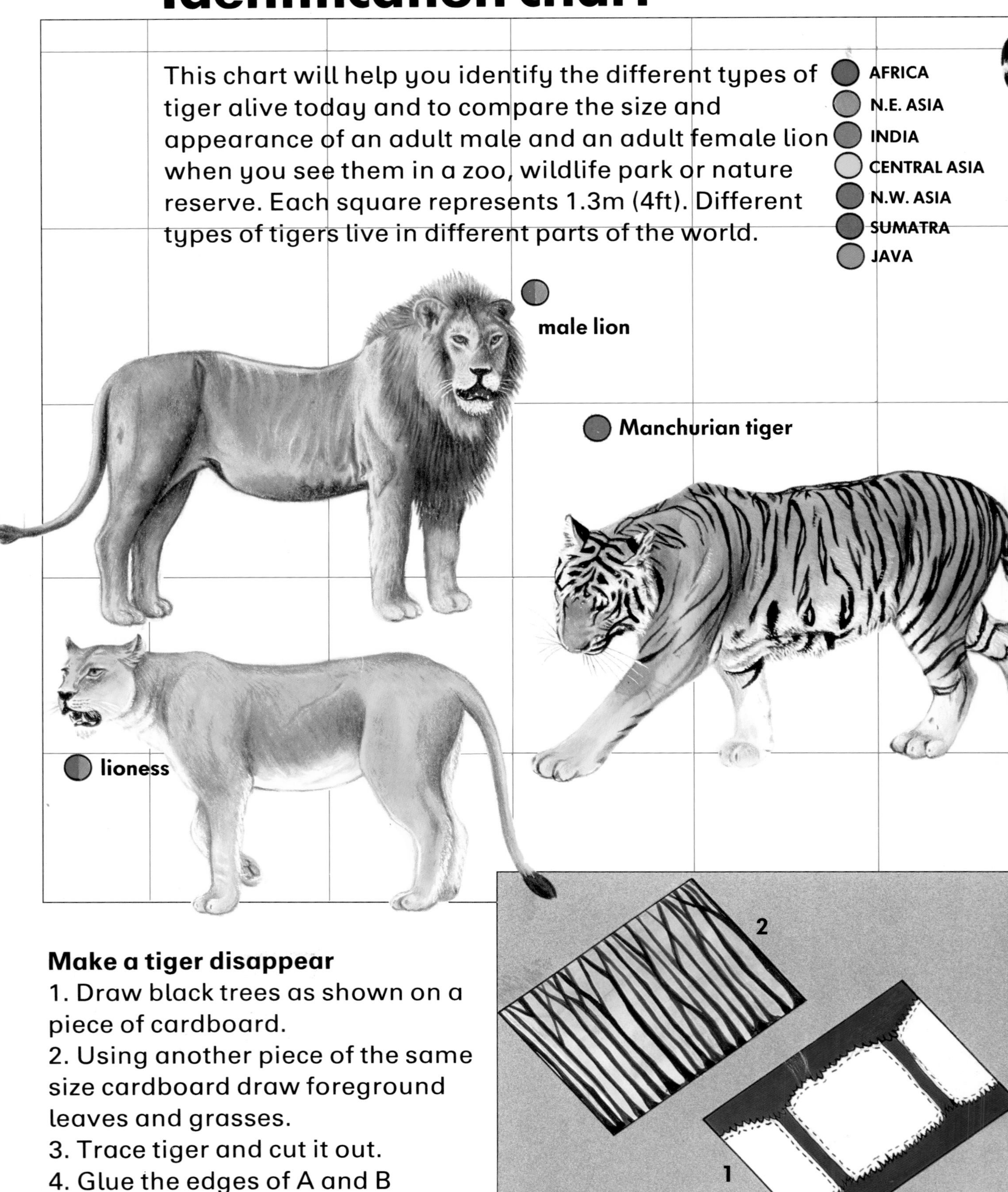


**Make a tiger disappear**

1. Draw black trees as shown on a piece of cardboard.
2. Using another piece of the same size cardboard draw foreground leaves and grasses.
3. Trace tiger and cut it out.
4. Glue the edges of A and B together as shown and insert C.
5. Pull tiger and watch it disappear.

Indian tiger
White tiger
Caspian tiger
Sumatran tiger
Javan tiger
A
3
4
glue
glue
C
B
5

# Index




**Photographic Credits**: Cover and pages 4, 17, 22, 24 and 25: Planet Earth; title page and pages 6, 8, 11, 13, 15, 19, 21, 26, 27, 28 and 29 (both): Bruce Coleman; page 23: Frank Spooner Agency.